Interview Workbook for Predoctoral Internships in Clinical Psychology

Heather Neill, Psy.D.

DEDICATION

To my mom who has, and always will be, my biggest supported and fan.

CONTENTS

ACKNOWLEDGMENTS

I would like to express my gratitude and appreciation to Lisa Lilenfeld,
Ph.D. and Sheila Williamson, Ph.D., both of whom guided and supported
me throughout my time as a doctoral student and predoctoral intern.
Thank you for believing in me.

1 AIRLINE & RENTAL CAR INFORMATION

Airline Frequent Flier Membership Numbers

Alaska Airlines:

American Airlines:

Delta Air Lines:

JetBlue:

Southwest Airlines:

Spirit Airlines:

United Airlines:

US Airways:

Other:

Other:

Rental Car Membership / Rewards Numbers

Alamo:

Avis:

Budget:

Dollar:

Enterprise:

Hertz:

National:

Thrifty:

Other:

Other:

2 INTERNSHIP SITE & TRAVEL INFORMATION FOR 10 SITES

Internship Site #1

Name:

Address:

Date & Time of Interview:

Name & Information of Internship Contact:

Additional Info:

Travel Information

Flight

Airline:

Reservation Number:

Date & Time of Flight(s):

Rental Car Information

Rental Car Company:

Phone Number:

Reservation Number:

Pick-up & Drop-off Time(s):

Hotel Information

Name of Hotel:

Address:

Reservation Number:

Check-in & Check-out Time(s):

Internship Site #2

Name:

Address:

Date & Time of Interview:

Name & Information of Internship Contact:

Additional Info:

Travel Information

Flight

Airline:

Reservation Number:

Date & Time of Flight(s):

Rental Car Information

Rental Car Company:

Phone Number:

Reservation Number:

Pick-up & Drop-off Time(s):

Hotel Information

Name of Hotel:

Address:

Reservation Number:

Check-in & Check-out Time(s):

Internship Site #3

Name:

Address:

Date & Time of Interview:

Name & Information of Internship Contact:

Additional Info:

Travel Information

Flight

Airline:

Reservation Number:

Date & Time of Flight(s):

Rental Car Information

Rental Car Company:

Phone Number:

Reservation Number:

Pick-up & Drop-off Time(s):

Hotel Information

Name of Hotel:

Address:

Reservation Number:

Check-in & Check-out Time(s):

Internship Site #4

Name:

Address:

Date & Time of Interview:

Name & Information of Internship Contact:

Additional Info:

Travel Information

Flight

Airline:

Reservation Number:

Date & Time of Flight(s):

Rental Car Information

Rental Car Company:

Phone Number:

Reservation Number:

Pick-up & Drop-off Time(s):

Hotel Information

Name of Hotel:

Address:

Reservation Number:

Check-in & Check-out Time(s):

Internship Site #5

Name:

Address:

Date & Time of Interview:

Name & Information of Internship Contact:

Additional Info:

Travel Information

Flight

Airline:

Reservation Number:

Date & Time of Flight(s):

Rental Car Information

Rental Car Company:

Phone Number:

Reservation Number:

Pick-up & Drop-off Time(s):

Hotel Information

Name of Hotel:

Address:

Reservation Number:

Check-in & Check-out Time(s):

Internship Site #6

Name:

Address:

Date & Time of Interview:

Name & Information of Internship Contact:

Additional Info:

Travel Information

Flight

Airline:

Reservation Number:

Date & Time of Flight(s):

Rental Car Information

Rental Car Company:

Phone Number:

Reservation Number:

Pick-up & Drop-off Time(s):

Hotel Information

Name of Hotel:

Address:

Reservation Number:

Check-in & Check-out Time(s):

Internship Site #7

Name:

Address:

Date & Time of Interview:

Name & Information of Internship Contact:

Additional Info:

Travel Information

Flight

Airline:

Reservation Number:

Date & Time of Flight(s):

Rental Car Information

Rental Car Company:

Phone Number:

Reservation Number:

Pick-up & Drop-off Time(s):

Hotel Information

Name of Hotel:

Address:

Reservation Number:

Check-in & Check-out Time(s):

Internship Site #8

Name:

Address:

Date & Time of Interview:

Name & Information of Internship Contact:

Additional Info:

Travel Information

Flight

Airline:

Reservation Number:

Date & Time of Flight(s):

Rental Car Information

Rental Car Company:

Phone Number:

Reservation Number:

Pick-up & Drop-off Time(s):

Hotel Information

Name of Hotel:

Address:

Reservation Number:

Check-in & Check-out Time(s):

Internship Site #9

Name:

Address:

Date & Time of Interview:

Name & Information of Internship Contact:

Additional Info:

Travel Information

Flight

Airline:

Reservation Number:

Date & Time of Flight(s):

Rental Car Information

Rental Car Company:

Phone Number:

Reservation Number:

Pick-up & Drop-off Time(s):

Hotel Information

Name of Hotel:

Address:

Reservation Number:

Check-in & Check-out Time(s):

Internship Site #10

Name:

Address:

Date & Time of Interview:

Name & Information of Internship Contact:

Additional Info:

Travel Information

Flight

Airline:

Reservation Number:

Date & Time of Flight(s):

Rental Car Information

Rental Car Company:

Phone Number:

Reservation Number:

Pick-up & Drop-off Time(s):

Hotel Information

Name of Hotel:

Address:

Reservation Number:

Check-in & Check-out Time(s):

Internship Site (Extra)

Name:

Address:

Date & Time of Interview:

Name & Information of Internship Contact:

Additional Info:

Travel Information

Flight

Airline:

Reservation Number:

Date & Time of Flight(s):

Rental Car Information

Rental Car Company:

Phone Number:

Reservation Number:

Pick-up & Drop-off Time(s):

Hotel Information

Name of Hotel:

Address:

Reservation Number:

Check-in & Check-out Time(s):

3 INTERNSHIP INTERVIEW QUESTIONS

Tell me about yourself.

How did you become interested in psychology? How did you become interested in (specific interest area)?

What are your personal strengths and weaknesses? What have you done to deal with your shortcomings?

What are your goals after graduate school? In 5 years? 10 years?

What do you have to contribute to us?

Why should we accept you over other equally qualified candidates?

What do you do in your spare time (hobbies, self-care, etc.)?

Tell me about your interest in this area (geography)?

Why did you choose this career path?

Why did you apply to this internship site?

What are you looking for in a psychology internship?

What are your goals during internship? After internship?

What unique qualities would you bring to our training program?

What are your specific clinical interests?

What do you see as your professional strengths and areas for further development? How do they influence your work?

Describe your previous supervisory relationships and what you are expecting from supervision at your internship site.

What sorts of supervisors have you had? What type of supervision works/doesn't work for you?

Discuss a difficult supervision experience, including how it was resolved.

Describe your experience working with a multidisciplinary treatment team.

How do you think you will handle the workload? What strategies do you use to prevent yourself from getting overwhelmed?

How do you cope with pressure and deadlines?

What haven't I asked you that you think I should know about you?

What psychological tests are you familiar with?

What further assessment training or experiences do you need?

What is your opinion of projective techniques?

What Rorschach scoring system do you use? Why?

What do you think of this Rorschach response?

What is your opinion of MMPI-2?

Comment on this MMPI profile.

How do you describe your therapeutic style?

What is your greatest strength as a therapist?

What further therapy training or experiences do you need?

What is your theoretical orientation in therapy? What do you think of (psychodynamic, CBT, behavioral, integrative, etc.) approaches?

What types of empirically supported treatments are you familiar with?

Describe your approach to case conceptualization.

Conceptualize a recent case (or a case presented to you as a vignette). Be prepared to discuss a case on the fly or a case you previously prepared.

Describe your experiences providing (family, group, inpatient, etc.) treatment.

Describe a case that went particularly well. Why?

Describe a case that did not go so well. Why? What would you do differently?

Have you worked with clients such as the ones we have here?

How do you work with and understand people with different ethnic or cultural backgrounds?

What sorts of clients have you worked with? Which were you most comfortable with? Which were you least comfortable with? Which were you most effective with?

What type of client is most difficult for you to work with? What type of feelings do you have toward such cases? How do these feelings interfere with your treatment?

What aspects of your personality most affect your work with patients?

Are there any patient populations with which you cannot work?

Tell me about an ethical problem you have been faced with and how you handled it.

When would/should a psychologist break confidentiality?

Have you ever broken confidentiality with a patient? If so, describe the circumstances.

What are your research interests? How did you get interested in this topic?

What is the clinical relevance of your research?

What is the status of your dissertation?

What research do you want to pursue here?

4 QUESTIONS TO ASK

Professional/Interview Staff

What are you looking for in an intern?

What interested you in my application?

What does an intern do during a typical work week?

What do you think the strengths of this internship are?

What do you think makes your internship program unique from other similar programs?

Are interns on call after hours? If so, how does this work?

What office resources are available to interns? (e.g., computers, own office, etc.)

Are any changes in stipends or benefits expected?

Does funding for the program depend on fees generated by the interns and staff?

What types of positions do your interns typically take after internship?

Can you tell me more about the _____ rotation?

Do you anticipate any changes in the rotations being offered next year?

How are cases and group assigned? Do interns have a say in assignments?

Current Interns

What does a typical workday or workweek look like for an intern?

How many hours per week are you required to work? Do you take work home with you?

Are you on call after hours? If so, how does this work?

Do you have your own office? Telephone extension? Voice mail? Access to a computer?

How many assessment batteries are required?

What rotations do you regard as being truly outstanding? Which ones should you avoid?

Which supervisors are most supportive of learning and which ones should we watch out for?

How would you describe the quality of supervision? Do you get enough hours?

How are interns treated by staff?

Do you feel supported by the faculty here?

How do interns get along here?

Have you had any regrets about accepting this position?

Have you enjoyed living in the area? What kinds of things are there to do?

What is the cost of living in this area?

What was the most difficult thing to adjust to when you first started internship?

When you were interviewing last year, is there anything that you didn't ask that you think would have been important to know?

How well is this internship preparing you for licensure and postdoc?

ABOUT THE AUTHOR

Dr. Heather Neill earned a masters and doctorate in clinical psychology, followed by a formal postdoctoral fellowship in forensic psychology. She is most passionate about providing services to individuals suffering from severe and persistent mental illness who are also involved in the legal system. Dr. Neill has worked in both state and federal prisons, as well as state and forensic hospitals, and the Courts. Most recently, Dr. Neill began a YouTube series entitled, "Becoming a Psychologist," which is geared towards individuals who are interested in pursuing a career in psychology or the mental health profession.

www.ingramcontent.com/pod-product-compliance
Lightning Source LLC
Chambersburg PA
CBHW070747240726
48654CB00010B/1201